A COMPARISON OF POETRY
AND MUSIC

A
COMPARISON OF POETRY
AND MUSIC

BY

SIR W. H. HADOW

THE
HENRY SIDGWICK LECTURE
1925

CAMBRIDGE
AT THE UNIVERSITY PRESS
1926

CAMBRIDGE
UNIVERSITY PRESS

University Printing House, Cambridge CB2 8BS, United Kingdom

Cambridge University Press is part of the University of Cambridge.

It furthers the University's mission by disseminating knowledge in the pursuit of education, learning and research at the highest international levels of excellence.

www.cambridge.org
Information on this title: www.cambridge.org/9781316509548

© Cambridge University Press 1926

First published 1926
First paperback edition 2015

A catalogue record for this publication is available from the British Library

ISBN 978-1-316-50954-8 Paperback

A COMPARISON OF
POETRY & MUSIC

I HAVE chosen this subject for the reason which animated the Cambridge apprentice in Moore's Diary. Anxious to enlarge his mental horizon he set himself, in such time as he could spare, to attend the public lectures of the University, beginning with those of the Professor of Greek. When he was asked why he had made this choice he replied that in other subjects, such as History or Modern Literature, he might be at a disadvantage confronted with men of greater knowledge than his own: "Here, however," he added, with a glance round which included the lecturer, "here, I presume that we are all much on the same level." That is how I feel this afternoon. I am certain that there are some very interesting things to be said about the comparison of music and poetry; about the resemblances and diversities of their appeal; but I do not know what they are: I am still groping after them. So I am here not to prescribe, but to suggest, not to indicate, but to search, and since it takes two to speak the truth, the greater part of that function will be yours.

"If music and sweet poetry agree," says Richard Barnfield, and never doubts that they do—

As they must needs, the sister and the brother—

laying a sure foundation for that comparison between Dowland and Spenser which to many of us at the present day sounds so remote and unfamiliar:

One god is god of both, as poets feign:

not, you will observe, "as musicians feign": it is from the side of poetry that the welcome is offered. And a generation later we find John Milton, the poet, writing to his father, John Milton, the madrigalist:

Nunc tibi quid mirum si me genuisse poetam
Contigerit, charo si jam prope sanguine juncti,
Cognatas artes, studiumque adfine sequamur?
Ipse volens Phoebus se dispertire duobus,
Altera dona mihi, dedit altera dona parenti:
Dividuumque Deum genitorque puerque tenemus.

"Cognatas artes"—"sphere-born har-
monious sisters, voice and verse." Nor
should we feel any surprise that Milton
writes in this manner. Of all poets up
to our present Laureate he is the one
whose understanding of music is most
complete and accurate: from the days
of his boyhood, when he commemo-
rates Adrian Batten's playing at St
Paul's, to the days of his old age when
he found in the organ his chief solace
and delight, he dwelt in the inner
courts of musical art, his gift of clear
and exact presentation never fails him
even in this most elusive of subjects[1].
For two centuries, indeed, our music
and our poetry were on terms of high
mutual regard. Dryden, who comes at the
end of the period, when the estrangement was already beginning, paid Pur-
cell a royal compliment in the preface
to *Amphitryon*, collaborated with him

---

[1] See, for instance, his description of a fugue,
Paradise Lost, xi, 561–3. It is, so far as I know, the
best in all literature.

over *King Arthur* and wrote in praise of music the ode which, with his accustomed candour he described as "the best that ever was or will be in the English language." Yet as we read *Alexander's Feast* our misgivings begin: music is treated only for its emotional effect, its power of rousing or assuaging passion: there is too much about Jove and Bacchus and the Trojan ghosts and the burning of the palace: the poet stands outside his theme, not as Milton does at its very heart and centre. And in the next generation the breach widened. With the exception of Arbuthnot our Annians were either indifferent to music or antagonistic: Pope, who actively disliked it, wrote his *Ode on St Cecilia's Day* with manifest reluctance: and, though we may admire the smoothness of its phrase and the skill of its versification, we must remember that it was held of little account in its own time, and that it remained for a hundred and fifty years an unlit lantern until it was

illuminated at last by the genius of Sir
Hubert Parry.

So through the eighteenth and early
nineteenth centuries the estrangement
continued. Music fades away from the
works of our English poets: Wordsworth, Coleridge, Southey, are outside
its influence; Shelley "pants for the
music which is divine" but shows no
comprehension of it; Byron has little
to show except the songs that he wrote
for Braham, Keats has virtually nothing.
Nor was France any the more sympa-
thetic. No doubt it made a political
quarrel out of the "Guerre des Bouf-
fons," but there were too many com-
peting issues for this to count as
evidence: Rousseau had some music in
him, but Voltaire had none, nor had
Chénier: Victor Hugo's one tribute to
Beethoven[1] is not more helpful than

[1] Note to *Les Châtiments*. The "admirable musique
de Beethoven" there quoted is a mutilated version
of a poor melody, very doubtfully attributed to
Beethoven and quite unworthy of him.

Gautier's famous definition of music as "le plus désagréable de tous les sons."

But the most salient instance is yet to relate. For nearly sixty years Goethe may almost be said to have represented the mind of Germany. During the period of its greatest intellectual activity he led nearly every advance: poetry, drama, fiction; the criticism of literature, of pictorial art, of architecture; optics, metaphysics, biology, studies of social conditions in his own and other countries; it would seem at first sight as if there were no topic in the whole range of human intelligence to which he did not offer welcome and hospitality. When he was born J. S. Bach was still alive: before he died Schumann had begun the draft of his first symphony. Within his lifetime falls the entire work of Haydn, Mozart, Beethoven, Schubert, Weber. What, we may ask, has the greatest of Germans to say about the greatest of German arts?

We are told that he was once moved

by *Zauberflöte* and conceived for a moment the idea of supplying it with a sequel: but the interest, to whatever cause attributable, was no more than a wave on the surface. We are told that in his old age he petted the young Mendelssohn, who must have been an extremely attractive child, but the two little poems which he exchanged for a dedication are among the weakest and least inspired of all his writings. Beethoven, with whom he was on terms of personal acquaintanceship, begged him to obtain from Karl August a subscription towards the printing of the *Missa Solennis:* Goethe refused. Schubert, the noblest of all his interpreters in music, sent him the manuscript of *Erlkönig.* Goethe returned no answer. And for the rest, though I speak under correction, I can recall no allusions to music in all that vast field of knowledge and research, except a perfunctory paragraph in the *Annalen*, mentioning some concerts in his house, a note in *Ferneres*

über Kunst about the founding of a new
Conservatorium, and a few sentences of
operatic criticism in which he joins together the names of Mozart and Cima-
rosa.

To trace all the causes of this gradual
alienation, even if it were possible,
would carry us beyond the limits of our
theme. But one reason may be sug-
gested, of which both the obverse and
the reverse appear equally significant.
In the late sixteenth and early seven-
teenth centuries, the time of our madri-
galists and song writers, the vast pre-
ponderance of music was vocal and the
poet looked to it as the natural comrade
and illustration of his own art. Shakespear combines with Morley, Lawes
with Milton: the sphere-born harmo-
nious sisters are singing, as Helena says,
"both in one key." But by the middle
of the eighteenth century the current
vocal form, outside the services of the
Church, was the conventional Italian
Opera which, during those years,

touched its lowest depth of degradation. Written at breakneck speed, on a
rigid and invariable plan, intended
only for an evening's entertainment
before an audience listless or preoccu-
pied, with no chance of being printed,
no hope of appealing to a wider public
and no prospect even of intelligent
criticism, it set up a monument of folly
from which literature very naturally
turned in disdain. At the beginning of
this period Addison complains that
" music renders us incapable of hearing
sense ": towards its end Miss Austen,
who in *Persuasion* devotes a chapter to
a concert without mentioning the music,
lays it down as unreasonable to look
for the meaning of an Italian love song.
At the same time the more serious com-
posers were beginning to discover and
administer an autonomous kingdom of
their own—the kingdom of suite and
partita, of sonata and quartet, of con-
certo and symphony, into which the
collaboration of the poet was not in-

vited. It is intelligible, it is almost inevitable, that the poet should look upon this new art with impatience: with the laws of its structure he was not conversant, the sound of its voice was pleasant but the speech was inarticulate: it seemed to be always hovering on the edge of a thought which as constantly melted away in the utterance. To such a man, "Sonate, que veux-tu?" is a perfectly natural question, and though we may shelter ourselves for a moment behind the famous mathematician who, after seeing a play of Racine, asked, "Et qu'est-ce que cela prouve?" yet we feel that the poet's question is relevant and that it must be answered. What is the significance of music and how is it related to the significance of poetry?

And first we may note that these two arts have a common ground which places them at once in direct antithesis to painting and sculpture and architectural design. They are essentially temporal arts, depending for their apprehension on a fixed and determinate succession. We may see the composition of a picture as a whole: we can study its detail from right to left or from left to right, upwards or downwards, as we choose. But with a melody or a sentence all this is impossible: the experience is not complete, is not even fully intelligible, until the last word or the last note, and the order of its recurrence is irreversible. Take the most familiar line of Shakespear, the most familiar tune of Handel, and try to repeat it backwards: you cannot do so, and it would have no meaning if you did. This implies a resemblance between these arts the importance of which cannot be over-estimated—that they are both continually throwing your attention forward, that at each moment in their course they are rousing the anticipation which it is their aim finally to satisfy. It is, therefore, a point of skill to bring before the hearer com-peting issues, to set him wondering; now to stimulate him with an effect of surprise, now to let him come to the edge of the solution and help him across; now, and this is best of all, to show him that the true issue was implicit all the time, and that the climax is its organic and inevitable conclusion. No doubt this quality may sometimes be turned to trivial account—some mere clench or conceit, some device of "keeping the easy rhymes till the end": none the less it is present throughout and it rises to its highest in the supreme moments of structural design. The dull speaker, the dull poet, the dull musician either lets his point be anticipated or buries it in anti-climax: the real artist in words or notes keeps his denouement in reserve so that it strikes the more keenly because the blow has been withheld.

Let me give you one or two instances. And though it is poetry which we are here comparing with music I would ask leave to take the first from rhetoric because it gives the clearest illustration that I know of this quality expressed in its simplest terms. It is a sentence from Cicero's *Pro Milone*:

Domi suae nobilissimus vir, senatus propugnator atque illis quidem temporibus paene patronus, avunculus hujus nostri judicis M. Catonis, fortissimi viri, tribunus plebis, M. Drusus occisus est.

Observe with what forensic skill this sentence is built up. "Domi suae"—something happened at somebody's house; "nobilissimus vir"—evidently a person of consequence; "senatus propugnator atque patronus"—of great consequence; "avunculus hujus nostri judicis"—that brings it home: let me see, who was Cato's uncle?; "tribunus plebis"—of course I know now; and just as the hearer's mind leaps forward to the tragedy of the great tribune, Cicero meets him with that clash of sibilants, like a serpent in act to strike— "M. Drusus occisus est"—Marcus Drusus was assassinated.

Take a quieter but equally famous instance from the ninth book of *Paradise Lost*:

> As one who, long in populous city pent,
> Where houses thick and sewers annoy the air,
> Forth issuing on a summer's morn to breathe
> Among the pleasant villages and farms
> Adjoin'd, from each thing met conceives delight,
> The smell of grain, or tedded grass, or kine,
> Or dairy, each rural sight, each rural sound;
> If chance with nymph-like step fair virgin pass,
> What pleasing seem'd, for her now pleases more,
> She most, and in her look sums all delight.[1]

" Annoy," " summer's morn," " pleasant," all preparing for the change from the noisome town to the fresh country air: then the delicious landscape unfolds (how perfect a picture in how few words) and at its close the girl crosses the meadow and completes the scene with a touch of human beauty and human sympathy.

One more example in which the effect is produced by contrast:

[1] Compare, for a different kind of structure, on the same theme, Keats' sonnet "As one who hath been long in city pent."

When in disgrace with fortune and men's eyes
  I all alone beweep my outcast state,
And trouble deaf Heaven with my bootless cries,
  And look upon myself and curse my fate,

—and so Shakespear continues, glooming through dark minor keys till he comes to that worst pitch of misery where a man despises his own unhappiness; and then, in the space of a crotchet, in the turn of a semitone, the sonnet changes from minor to major, like a shaft of sunlight through an unbarred window—

Haply I think of thee, and then my state
(Like to the lark at break of day arising
  From sullen earth) sings hymns at Heaven's gate:
For thy sweet love remembered such wealth brings
That then I scorn to change my state with kings.

"Heaven" and "state" occur both at the beginning and at the end of the sonnet: but in the two places they are differently harmonised. All through good music there runs this quality of projected attention. Take any great choral tune, *Ein Feste Burg*, or *Nun Danket*, or *Moab*: any folk-song like *The*

Bailiff's Daughter, or *Early one morning*, any typical melody of Beethoven or Schubert—the Romance in *Rosamunde*, the *Ständchen*, the slow-movement tunes of the *Pathétique* or the *Pastoral* or the late E major Sonata—and note how the beauty and interest of this texture is heightened and enhanced as they approach their cadence. The same is true of composition on a larger canvas—the end of *Tristan* and of *Meistersinger*, the hurricane of the *Appassionata*, the closing miracle of the *Jupiter* Symphony. This does not, of course, mean any such absurdity as that all great music or poetry is a profusion of climaxes: that would obviously defeat its own end and ensure its own downfall. Everything depends on the unit of attention which may be a stanza or an ode, an eight-bar melody or a symphonic movement. It may be a necessary part of the suspense that some passages should be kept at a low pitch: it must be a necessary part that the device is never obtrusive or mechanical, but grows in its place as naturally as a flower: in any case the temporal condition is paramount and the great artist has accepted it and has used it not as a restriction, but as a resource.

Another point of likeness may be noted. Tone and rhythm, which are metaphors, though valuable metaphors, in the representative arts, are in music and poetry vital and essential realities. In both of these music would seem to have the advantage. It falls altogether outside the play and interchange of consonants (for all the letters in its alphabet are vowels) and on this side it is debarred from one of the most telling qualities of articulate speech. But this is compensated, and it may be more than compensated, by the greater beauty of musical sound—the beauty which makes it the highest praise of a language that we should call it musical. I do not deny the moving tones of the great orator: I know that men have read Swinburne for the sheer delight of his verse; but it is no paradox to say that these fall below the resonance of the singing voice or the orchestra or the four magic strings. Music, again, is the only art which has the power of

> Untwisting all the chains that tie
> The hidden soul of harmony.

It alone can make "out of three sounds not a fourth sound but a star": that new creation achieved by the blending and absorbing of intermingled voices. Nor in rhythm is the supremacy of music less apparent. The Classical poets could work wonders by the counter-change of stress and quantity, but even with them the limit of variation is comparatively narrow. The moderns, who have all but lost this distinction, have attempted to replace it in various ways: the French by free play of sound within determinate systems of metre: the English and German by some lightness of additional syllables, as you may break up a crotchet into quavers, yet hampered throughout by the natural pace of the speaking voice. Coleridge, at the beginning of *Christabel*, deliberately introduced a new melody into English versification: Lamb declared that "a long line was a line which was long in reading," irrespective of the number of syllables that it contained: most notable of all in this field are the experiments which Dr Bridges has made in breaking up the conventional designs of his metre. Take, for instance, the poem called *London Snow*. The first line—

When men were all asleep the snow came flying,

sets a metre with which we have all been familiar since the opening of the *Canterbury Tales*. The second line begins a subtle variation:

In long white flakes falling on the city brown:

the third and fourth cluster with semi-quavers:

Stealthily and perpetually falling and loosely lying,
Hushing the latest traffic of the drowsy town.

It is not too much to say that these

lines mark an epoch in the history of English verse: yet when you compare them with their analogues in music—with any page of the *Fitzwilliam Virginal Book*, or of Bach's *Forty-eight*, or of Beethoven or Wagner or Brahms, you will see not the lesser skill of the poet, for he has gone as far as language can go, but the lesser flexibility of his medium. Or, again, take the device of syncopation, traversing the bar-metre by a stress thrown on a weak beat, most effective when rightly used, deplorably vulgarised at the present day: compare the finest examples in Milton—

> And over them triumphant death his dart
> Shook, but delayed to strike.

with the finest examples in Beethoven, as, for instance, in the first movement of the *Eroica*; the difference is not one of genius, but one of opportunity. Or, again, take the grouping and phrasing of notes "across the bar" as in A.E.'s couplet:

The gardens lull me, and the sound of many waters,
    and I hear
Familiar voices, and the voice I love is whispering in
    my ear.

A miracle, you will say, wrought by three commas; transforming a commonplace metre into a new and living melody. In terms of language it cannot be better done. But contrast it with the lyric movement of Brahms' G minor quartet and you see what genius can achieve, in this manner, with a more responsive instrument at command.

On the other side there can be no doubt that poetry is far more precise and direct than music. One of the most notable qualities of the great Epic writers, especially of Dante and Milton, is their power of presenting the object as it is, of placing it before us in concrete shape and substance. This does not mean that they copy phenomena, any more than the landscape painter copies nature, but that they crystallise round phenomena the ideas that they hold in imagination. It is because they can

> See the world in a grain of sand,
> And Heaven in a wild flower,

that they can make the wild flower and the grain of sand real and significant: and one measure of their genius is the clearness with which they perceive the Idea and the certainty with which they embody it. Wordsworth saw the whole world "apparelled in celestial light," and therefore no detail of it escaped his vision. Shakespear comprehended all the archetypes of human character, and therefore his personages are as real to us as our familiar friends. But the phenomenal world is the vehicle through which the poet expresses his ideas, and because it is the world of our own experience it brings them into specially close and intimate relation with ourselves.

From this kind of reality music is excluded. It can suggest, but it cannot narrate: it can rouse our emotions but

it cannot specify them. A few sounds
and movements in nature can be more
or less imitated by its tones or rhythms;
these lie at the far outskirts and are of
no serious account. Descriptive music,
in the broader sense of the term, is at
best only a half-art, needing words or
a written programme or dramatic action
to prescribe its meaning. Even then it
should be "mehr Ausdruck der Emp-
findung als Malerei." Schubert, for
instance, makes no attempt in *Erlkönig* to
depict an actual storm—he gives us instead a vague general feeling of turbu-
lence and sinister flight: Wagner in the
prelude to *Walküre* begins with the same
musical theme as Schubert and writes
on it a fine stirring piece which falls
short of its purpose only so far as it
attempts to be realistic. *Heldenleben* has
a programme almost as close in detail
as that of the *Symphonie Fantastique*: he
would be a bold listener who should
endeavour to rewrite the story of either
from hearing the music. And in pro-

portion as music withdraws from the drama and the written programme, in proportion as it holds its own autonomous and independent course, so far it recedes from any meaning that could be translated into terms of any other experience. We may find plenty of analogues if we will, and they are often helpful and suggestive, but they are analogues, not interpretations.

Yet within its own domain music has a reality not less than that of any other art. The style of Bach is as perfect as that of Milton, the structure of Beethoven as that of Shakespear: bad music is, as Coleridge said, the exact equivalent of nonsense verses. But the significance of music is not related to anything outside itself; it is inherent in the succession of notes, the interweaving of parts, the design of themes, contrasted or recurrent, throughout a piece of composition. In all other arts, even in poetry, we can make some sort of abstraction between form and content: in the best

music we cannot, they are fused and
absorbed into one supreme act of creation. When we hear the slow movement
of the Choral Symphony we are not
conscious of any specific joy or sorrow,
still less of any scene or event: the spell
of that enchantment is beyond the reach
of any words.

This is, I think, what Schopenhauer
means by the famous analysis of Art
which occupies Book III of the *World as
Will and Idea*. There are, he tells us, four
kinds or degrees of apprehension. First,
the empirical in which we are aware of
phenomena merely as isolated facts and
merely in relation to our own will, that
is to the use that we can make of them.
Next in order comes the scientific (in
Bacon's sense of the term) which so
correlates phenomena as to infer, ac-
cording to the principle of sufficient
reason, those general laws which, to the
apprehending mind, are *universalia post
rem*. Next above this come the representative arts (including poetry up to

its highest manifestation in the Tragic drama), the genius of which consists "in the capacity for knowing, independently of the principle of sufficient reason, not individual things which exist only in their relations, but the Idea of such things, and of being oneself the correlative of the Idea and thus no longer an individual but the pure subject of knowledge."[1] It must, of course, be understood that Schopenhauer is using the term Idea in the Platonic sense, which accentuates the discrepancy between this view and the degradation of art (as "the copy of a copy") in the tenth book of the *Republic*. A doctrine more in sympathy with that here enunciated may be found in the *Phaedrus* and at the beginning of the *Parmenides*. Finally, "Music is by no means like the other arts, the copy of the Ideas, but the copy of the Will itself, whose objectivity the Ideas are. This is why the effect of music is so much more power-

[1] *World as Will and Idea*, Book III, Section 37.

ful and penetrating than that of the other arts, for they speak only of shadows, but it speaks of the thing itself."[1] Schopenhauer puts this bluntly and vehemently—the Platonic Ideas cannot rightly be described as shadows, even for purposes of antithesis—but his distinction is clear. All other arts derive their content from the celestial hierarchy of Ideas: Music alone penetrates to the Presence beyond. Thus of all arts Music is the purest and the most philosophical: "exercitium metaphysices occultum nescientis se philosophari animi."

We must not press this definition as if it were exhaustive. In point of meaning Music may no doubt penetrate to a metaphysical world which is behind even the Ideal: so far as vehicle is concerned it needs the ear as avenue, and sound adapted to the ear as medium. There is at the present time a dangerous heresy called Expressionism, which is

[1] *World as Will and Idea,* Book III, Section 52.

threatening to invade the domains both of pictorial and of musical art. Its chief principle is, as its upholders tell us, "the denial of the sensible world." It is "indifferent to every perception of sense, and turns away from the outward world in order to behold with the eye of the spirit." This is false mysticism. No doubt Blake is abundantly right in saying:

> We are led to believe a lie
> When we see with, not through, the eye:

still more, perhaps, when we hear with, not through, the ear: but we must see and hear through these organs, they are the natural correlatives of sound and colour. And I notice with some misgiving that the plea of expressionism is commonly used to explain pictures which are apparently ugly, poetry which is apparently unmeaning and music which is apparently cacophonous. One cannot help thinking that the claims of sense, not as tribunal but as witness, are being here too little regarded. "Heard

melodies are sweet, but those unheard
are sweeter." I wonder whether that is
always the case. What says the clown
in *Othello*? " If you have any music
that may not be heard, to't again: but
as they say, to hear music the general
does not greatly care."

Another point of resemblance between
poetry and music is that they are specially liable to the same diseases. In
dealing with this matter I would ask
to leave on one side that deliberate
cult of ugliness for its own sake, which
stands to art as devil worship to Re-
ligion, and of which the present age
has been sometimes accused. It is too
serious an accusation to be discussed or
considered in the course of a brief and
general survey; if it is true it means not
disease but death, its basis is probably
some form of physiological pervasion,
and its proper field of investigation is
not Aesthetics but Pathology. Apart
from this, however, there are two
maladies which attack the temporal

arts with particular virulence, usually at
the end of some period of conspicuous
achievement. The first of these is
anarchy: the claim of a personal free-
dom which means flat defiance of all
law and all regulation. It is not experiment or adventure, which indeed are
the conditions of all progress, but blind
adventure and experiment conducted at
random. For the most part it belongs
to the recklessness of youth, and therefore deserves our cordial sympathy; but
it is no more a form of art than window-
breaking is a form of architecture. Some
remarkable instances are provided in
Trotzky's *Literature and Revolution*:
a book which must be absorbingly
interesting to those who have followed
the recent course of letters in Russia:
and which even to those who read it
without this knowledge is very significant. It describes Gorki as "an
amiable psalm-singer"; it treats Blok
as a Conservative; it is filled dispas-
sionately with accounts of authors,

some of whom are genuine pathfinders while others are dancing round and round in the wildest extravagance. One school is avoiding the charge of voluptuousness by writing its poetry in mathematical formulae; another is inventing nonsense-words like " Dir " and " Tschil " and maintaining that the patterns into which they can be wrought " strike a deeper note than anything in Pushkin." This is really worse than the literary machine which Gulliver saw at Lagado, for that at least employed real words, and their fortuitous concourses were dictated only when "they were such as might form parts of a sentence."

There are dozens of parallel instances in music. I possess at home a copy of a pianoforte sonata in which certain passages are to be played with the fist (presumably on some one else's piano) and others, for which the fist is inadequate, with a wooden plank fourteen inches in length. It presents a very decorative picture to the eye; crotchets like bunches of grapes and minims like spikes of corn; but the sound of it is inconceivable and the sense, to me, non-existent. Again, there are several un-distinguished compositions which bid for notoriety by the insertion of in-appropriate or meaningless discords; "put in," like the barking hen of Dan Leno's riddle, "to make it more diffi-cult." They are fairly on a level with the "transferred epithet" by which something which can have no colour, like a perfume, is called "black," some-thing which can have no perfume, like a triangle, is called "fragrant," and something which can have no shape, like Wednesday morning, is called "isosceles." It is the more vexing be-cause a great deal of first-rate pioneer work is being done at the present day, work of real genius and accomplished skill, enlarging the bounds of our musical vocabulary and creating new and beautiful forms. If some of our young people would give up cele-

brating the fifth of November and take
their place, beside their comrades, in
the general advance, they would be
aiding instead of disregarding the cause
of music.

A worse fault is pedantry—the fault of
those who are so over-weighted with
learning that they lose all sense of proportion in employing it. Of this the
classical instance is Lycophron, the
erudite librarian of Alexandria, whose
one surviving poem, a monologue of
Cassandra on the fall of Troy, is a
lamentable monument of misplaced
labour. He has heaped metaphor on
metaphor, obscurity on obscurity, he
has searched the dictionary for rare
words and the mythology for recondite
allusions—and he has produced in the
end a work of which he declared, with
all a scholar's pride, that "he would
hang himself if any one understood it."
Here is a comparatively easy passage:

I see the winged firebrand rushing to the capture
of the dove, the Pephnian hound, whom the water-

faring vulture brings to birth, enoystered in the sphere of a shell.[1]

"Enoystered": one can imagine the chuckle of delight with which he wrote down that remarkable word. But it takes some investigation to realise that what the lines mean is "I see Paris coming to capture Helen."

There is a passage in Schönberg's *Pierrot Lunaire* which seems exactly to match this. Piccolo and clarinet are playing in close canon at the distance of a quarter of a bar: violin and 'cello are playing a canon cancrizans on a new theme: the piano is playing a three part fugue on the theme of the first canon in augmentation : and the voice is narrating that when Pierrot walks in the cool of the evening the moon makes a white spot on his back. If all this display of counterpoint was successful it would overlay the tiny subject on which

[1] Λεύσσω θέοντα γρυνὸν ἐπτερωμένον
τρήρωνος εἰς ἅρπαγμα, Πεφναίας κυνός,
ἣν τόργος ὑγρόφοιτος ἐκλοχεύεται,
κελυφάνου στρόβιλον ὠστρακωμένην.

it is imposed: as a matter of fact it is
so involved that the ear cannot follow
it, and it makes no compensation in
beauty of sound. But, indeed, much of
our counterpoint is become so elaborate
that it no longer harmonises: "the dis-
sonances" we are told "are inherent in
the progression of parts and therefore
inevitable." It never seems to occur to
the composer that he might conciliate
the parts.

Sometimes the learned scholar be-
comes adventurous: starting with set
purpose and firm resolve to follow the
lure of the will-o'-the-wisp novelty.
I have never seen *Die Glückliche Hand* and
have therefore no right to express an
opinion on it. But I may perhaps be
allowed to summarise an account of its
opening scene, written by one of its
ablest and most devoted admirers.[1] At
the rise of the curtain the stage is in
almost complete darkness. Near the

[1] See the volume on Schönberg by Dr Egon
Wellesz, *s.v.*

front a man is lying face downwards. On his back is " a large cat-like animal" which "appears to have just bitten him in the neck." At the back of the stage is a violet curtain with twelve holes in it: through these appear the "greenish faces" of six men and six women who fulfil " the same function as that of the chorus in a Greek Tragedy." Half-speaking and half-singing they "express their sympathy for the man who has desired earthly happiness and has been given supernatural happiness instead."

This is what comes of " schools " and " movements " and " coteries " and all the other devices for tempting men into affectation. Sir Arthur Quiller-Couch once implored you to remember that no abstract noun ending in -ism had ever done anything or made anything or exercised any influence. If I may say so, I entirely agree with him. But I would go further. No one whose designation ends in -ist has, by reason of this, ever done anything or made

anything or exercised any influence
either. When I see their serried ranks
advancing, bent as a rule on some plan
for the annoyance of the aged, I com-
fort myself with the legend of St
Anthony: not the romantic mediaeval
form, beloved of painters, but the
original story as told by Athanasius.
The saint was lying ill on the mat of
palm-leaves which served him for a
bed, and the enemy of mankind thought
this a favourable opportunity for attack. So he sent a number of his fol-
lowers disguised as animals—wolf and
lion and tiger and snake and many others
—who entered the cell and proceeded
to make menacing noises. The saint
said two wise words: first, "If you were
real, one of you would be enough;"
and then, after they had become further
infuriated, "If it be the Lord's will that
you should bite me, come and do it; if
not, depart."

No reasonable person wishes to check
or discourage the advance. Such a wish

would be crabbed, for the advance is young, and futile, for it is irresistible. Mrs Partington had no chance, and ought to have known that she had no chance, against the Atlantic Ocean; "She was excellent at a slop or a puddle, but should not have meddled with a tempest." Yet it may be claimed that part of the function of criticism is to distinguish between the puddle and the ocean; between the shallow little fashion which will have dried up to-morrow, and the unplumbed depths of genius which will last for ever. And this function, if it is to be of any service, it must accomplish betimes. It is no use deferring arbitration until the parties have left the court.

It seems to me that there are two general principles of criticism which may help to guide our judgment of all arts and especially, perhaps, of the two with which we have been dealing this afternoon. One is that the continuity of human history and human civilisation is not broken, but fulfilled, by the advent of genius. The great artists are supreme not because they are freaks or usurpers, but because they stand in the royal line of succession : " nature," no doubt, " made them and then broke the mould; " but to the making of that mould went the work of many generations. There were contrapuntists before Bach, dramatists before Shakespear, ballad makers before Homer himself : each leader is the follower of a past tradition and by his own genius turns it to fresh account. The maxim " non facit saltum " is as true of Art as of Nature : each of them, for all its infinite variety, finds somewhere in the past the roots of the present and the future.

The other principle, on which one cannot too often lay stress, is that every art has its natural medium and every medium its natural qualities and limitations. The exact placing of these must from time to time be matter of controversy : we should not, I suppose, at

the present day accept all the conclu-
sions of the *Laocoon*, though some of
us might, in challenging them, feel a
doubt as to whether Lessing were not
right after all. Yet even within the
bounds of a single generic art we recog-
nise that the distinctions are real: the
architect does not apply the same design
to wood and brick and marble, and we
all know what Whistler thought of the
critic whose praise of a water-colour
was that he might have taken it for an
oil-painting. And so between the sister
arts of music and poetry—

Facies non omnibus una,
Nec diversa tamen, quales decet esse sororum:

the points of resemblance do not ex-
clude but invite the points of difference:
one interprets the ideal world through
phenomenal nature, the other need bor-
row nothing from nature but the sound
which is at once its subject and its
material. Poetry transfigures the world
of experience; music stands apart from
it: in the form of their presentation

they are akin, in the substance of that
which is presented they are separate. It
is true that at the supreme moments of
both they stand close together upon the
summit, but they climb to it from different sides, and if either takes the path
of the other it will lose its way.

www.ingramcontent.com/pod-product-compliance
Ingram Content Group UK Ltd.
Pitfield, Milton Keynes, MK11 3LW, UK
UKHW042141280225
455719UK00001B/11